# Those Old Placid Rows

## The Aesthetic and Development of the Baltimore Rowhouse

### Natalie W. Shivers

## MACLAY & ASSOCIATES INC.

Baltimore/1981

*"[The 18th century] invented the first really comfortable human habitations ever seen on earth, and filled them with charming fittings. . . The 18th century dwelling house has countless rivals today, but it is far superior to any of them as the music of Mozart is superior to Broadway jazz. It is not only, with its red brick and white trim, a pattern of simple beauty; it is also durable, relatively inexpensive, and pleasant to live in. No other sort of house better meets the exigencies of housekeeping, and none other absorbs modern conveniences more naturally and gracefully. Why should a man of today abandon it for a house of harsh masses, hideous outlines and bald metallic surfaces?. . .I can find no reason in either faith or morals. The 18th century house fits a civilized man almost perfectly. He is completely at ease in it. In every detail it accords with his ideas.[1]"*

— H. L. Mencken.

# Preface

*Those Old Placid Rows,* the title of this book, is borrowed from praise for Baltimore rowhouses by a famous native son, the writer H. L. Mencken. It suits a book that tells about the origins and development of these unassertive dwellings and about their special beauty. Moreover, Baltimoreans, like Mencken, can derive satisfaction from having created such fine architecture in their rows.

My goal is to foster appreciation of these rowhouses. For too long travelers have dismissed them as monotonous. But now the enthusiasm for urban living and for recycling old buildings is generating curiosity about cityscapes of the past. This curiosity is being met by this story of why Baltimore has so many rowhouses and why they look so much alike.

For Baltimoreans, of course, the streets of red brick with white trim, softened with green trees, look exactly the way a liveable city should. The typical rowhouse of the 19th and early 20th centuries looked enough like its 18th century English forebears to please the hard-to-please Mencken in 1931 and functions neatly enough to prove an ideal city residence in the 1980's.

Many people helped me with this book, and I am grateful to them all. My mother, Lottchen Vondersmith Shivers, and my father, Frank Remer Shivers, Jr., urged me to choose this topic for my senior thesis at Yale, and they have sustained me all the way through publication. My advisor, Professor David Cast, was amiably encouraging, and an authority on Maryland architecture, Michael F. Trostel, gave information and aid generously. Other facts and materials came cheerfully from John Dorsey, Charles Duff, Jr., Robert Eney, Douglas Gordon, Barbara Hoff, Wilbur Hunter, Jacques Kelly, Romaine Somerville, and the list goes on.

Collections of books and manuscripts that I consulted include those at the Yale School of Art and Architecture, the Library of Congress, Winterthur, the New York Public Library, Enoch Pratt Free Library, the Maryland Historical Society, and the Johns Hopkins University. The Peabody Library on Mount Vernon Place deserves a special bow for the kind interest of the librarian, Lynne Hart. My thanks also go to institutions who allowed my use of pictures and quotations.

Kevin Lippert, Ellen Watson Eager, and Pat Lauber Frost tried to make sure that the text made sense. Russell Monroe, Jr., Jerry Miller, and Judith A. Chamberlin gave up Sunday mornings to take pictures for these pages. And John Maclay, who designed and produced the book, combined our interests to issue this first volume in his series of books about Baltimore.

*View of Baltimore, 1850, by E. Sachse.*

# Part One

# The Aesthetic of the Baltimore Rowhouse

Every city has been confronted with the puzzle of fitting the most people into the least amount of space — preferably in a manner that is both comfortable and handsome. The usual solutions are apartment houses, which stack people horizontally, or rowhouses, which wedge people in vertically.

The rowhouse first appeared in Northern Europe. There the political and economic systems of England, Germany, and the Low Countries fostered a large middle class, whose concept of "home" was territorial.[2] Each family wanted its own doorstep—not one shared as apartment residents did theirs. The rowhouse suited this ideal without compromising efficient use of space. Because of the narrowness of the lots, each block accommodated many houses, while allowing everyone his own entrance.

After the English brought the rowhouse to America, most eastern cities housed people this way — at least for their first centuries. In spite of the historic role rowhouses have played in the design of America's cities, Americans today generally do not recognize the aesthetic value of rows. Many people do of course recognize how practical "townhouses" are. Traditionally, we have paid homage to the individual masterpiece, the single building. The attractions of groups of buildings that subordinate their individuality to an overall effect have gone unacknowledged. The long narrow lot of a rowhouse allows little variation in shape. But ensembles of rowhouses that offer a wide stretch of facade can be manipulated to take on grand proportions. Even when rows are not deliberately designed as an architectural composition, their contribution to the visual character of cities can be invaluable. Although often not special singly, rowhouses can be distinctive and handsome as groups, something recognized more in European than American cities.

For the cultural anthropologist, the rowhouse symbolizes the historical forces that shape a city. Every city produces its own variations on basic types of urban housing. These types bear the stamp of the region around them, taking on a different character according to the needs, tastes, and resources of each place. Because the basic form of a rowhouse — several stories high with two or more rooms per floor and a hall and stairway to one side — varies only slightly from region to region, local modifications are easily apparent. Many factors give each city's rowhouses a specific, identifiable character: local topography, climate, building codes, building materials, indigenous design traditions as well as non-local influences.

Although common to many American cities, particularly on the east coast, the rowhouse is Baltimore's special insignia. Local writers John Dorsey and James Dilts proclaimed:

*What the steel-frame high-rise is to Chicago, the lowly row house is to Baltimore. It provides the city's architectural ambiance, its character, and—with the legendary white marble steps—its claim to fame.*[3]

Baltimore's rowhouses are distinctive for four reasons: one, their abundance, for a visitor is probably more conscious of rowhouses in Baltimore than in any other American city; two, their architectural democracy, as they house all social classes; three, a distinctive aesthetic tradition based on forms and proportions rather than ornament; and four, the persistence of those qualities for over a century.

What most visitors find special about Baltimore's rows is the shape they give to the city: the straight even rows should have been monotonous as they undulate over the hills. But Baltimore's hills provide a counterpoint to the regular tempo of the rows, just as the rows give the hilly city its own peculiar visual rhythm. As architectural historian Vincent Scully writes:

*The beautiful streets of Baltimore, with their stone steps and fine doorways....show some of the best examples [of rowhouses]. The proportions are decisive; the buildings are high enough to give the street a shape, the doors and windows showing the scale of human use, the red brick of the defining walls varying in tone and therefore seeming to flow in and out down the street, the window cornices marking a beat, syncopating the rhythm, the major cornices giving the whole street shape a volumetric definition.* [4]

Known as the Monumental City, Baltimore early on developed a building tradition that took advantage of topography to site its monuments dramatically, as with the Washington Monument on Howard's Hill in 1815. Local builders constructed on a scale to rival and exaggerate the natural landscape. This manner of manipulating site and structure to complement each other carried over into the construction of rows as well:

the straight, flat silhouettes of the rowhouses created dramatic vistas and provided perfect settings for Baltimore's churches and monuments. The rows are distinguished without detracting from the distinction of the individual structures. Together, they enhance each other, and this pattern is how most visitors recognize Baltimore.

The next four sections present the aesthetic aspect of the Baltimore rowhouse — what it looks like and the factors responsible for its appearance.

# Georgian London Origins

*These narrow houses, three or four storeys high — one for eating, one for sleeping, a third for company, a fourth underground for the kitchen, a fifth perhaps at the top for servants — the agility, the ease, the quickness with which the individuals of the family run up and down, and perch on different storeys, give the idea of a cage with its sticks and birds.* [5]
— *Louis Simond, 1817*

*The terrace rows of Georgian London, like this one on Kennington Road built in the 1780's, represented the genesis of Baltimore's rows. Their classical proportions and sheer unornamented facades repeated en masse later became the basis of the Baltimore aesthetic.*

The rowhouse type used in Baltimore originated in Georgian London. Although Holland is credited with the invention of the rowhouse[6], it was the Georgian epoch in London that standardized and popularized the rowhouse form that is found on America's east coast.

While English middle class tastes demanded rowhouses rather than tenements, the economic incentive to fit as many houses as possible onto one street controlled the size and shape of the rowhouse. Urban and financial common sense dictated a structure that was narrow and high instead of wide and low. Verticality thus became the London idiom, while the populations of most continental capitals lived horizontally in apartment buildings.

The typical site was a long strip of ground: the front part covered by the house, the middle by the yard, the rear by a coach house or stable accessible by a subsidiary road. Generally, the narrowness of the lot prescribed a house plan composed of two rooms per floor, one at the front, one at the back, with a passage and staircase to one side. This plan was satisfactory for houses on broader sites as well, although other features were often added and the staircase repositioned to give these houses a more elegant character.

Like the layout, the basic configuration of the facade was a response to urban circumstances. It was almost as much a consequence of building regulations instituted after London's Great Fire in 1666 as of an architect's imagination. After the Fire, building acts abolished exposed woodwork, prominent eaves and cornices, and ruled that roofs should be hidden by parapet walls. At the same time, sash windows replaced casements. Thus, as it became more solid and compact, the facade was made regular and divested of ornament. The result was the standard Georgian brick house characterized by its planarity, order, and simplicity.

With these legal and spatial restrictions, a certain monotony of design would be expected. As James Fenimore Cooper complained in 1828, "The most that can be done with such a [narrow] front is to abstain from inappropriate ornament, and to aim at such an effect as shall convey a proper idea of the more substantial comforts, and of neatness that predominate within.'"

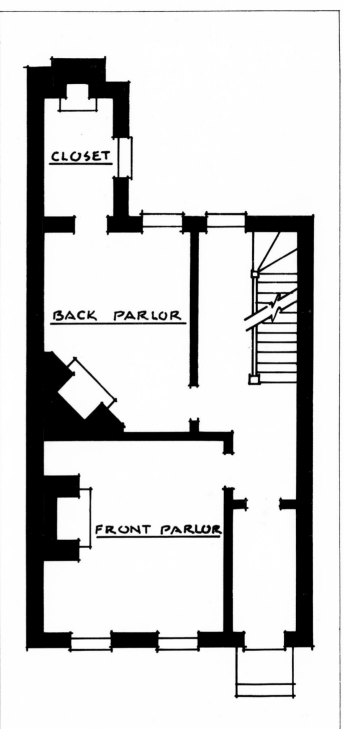

*The plan of the typical Georgian rowhouse, used from the late 17th until the mid-18th century, with a side hall and two rooms per floor, served as the prototype for the typical Baltimore rowhouse. (The "closet" was used as an office or even a bedroom. Dining rooms did not develop until after 1850.)*

When planned in groups, however, rowhouses were found to offer great possibilities for grand formal compositions. Planned rows trace back at least as far as Paris' Place des Vosges, constructed in 1610, which inspired Inigo Jones to repeat the "peas-in-a-pod" arrangement in 1630 at Covent Garden in London. Covent Garden in turn inspired a series of planned squares and streets in which individual dwellings were replaced by groups of dwellings planned as a unit.

Inigo Jones' Lindsay House at Lincoln's Inn Fields offers evidence of the design contributions his classicism made to London house fronts. The main principles found here were gradually distilled into popular domestic designs for rowhouses. The ideal Georgian facade presented a smooth broad plane with windows and ornament laid in a symmetrical composition of classical repose. Bricks were as regular as possible, so as not to distract the eye by creating a facade made up of many small busy units. The proportions and positions of windows were crucial, since they, rather than ornament, gave character to the Georgian facade and emphasized the important relationship between the interior hierarchy of spaces and the exterior.

Georgian proportions were based on the Italian tradition of the "piano nobile" and the concept of invisible applied orders. The ground story corresponded to the base, the piano nobile to the shaft, the chamber floor to the capital, and the attic story to the architrave of a column on the facade of a classical temple. The piano nobile, located on what Americans would consider the second story, was the primary floor; its rooms were the highest and, hence, the windows the tallest. Above that the size of windows diminished in proportion to their height on the building facade. Thus based on enduring classical principles as interpreted by Renaissance architects, Georgian proportions appeared harmonious and well-balanced.

Georgian taste demanded a serene, elegant effect, and these well-balanced rowhouse facades, which could be reproduced en masse, represented the ultimate expression of late 18th century classicism. Furthermore, personal expression on the part of the architect was regarded as irrelevant and academically unsound. This attitude was perfectly suited—both practically and aesthetically—to the terrace rows put up by speculators in this period. The simplicity and paucity of detail that appealed to the Georgian builder trying to increase his profit margin appealed equally to popular taste.

The style and configuration of the rowhouses of Georgian London served as the models for America's Federal rowhouses. Baltimore was particularly enamored with this style, and even the city's Victorian rowhouses reflect their Georgian roots.

*This row of mid- to late-18th century houses in Burlington, New Jersey, came out of the Philadelphia mold, which in turn was based on the terraces of Georgian London. The sphere of Philadelphia's influence on rowhouses extended as far north as Trenton, New Jersey and as far south as Georgetown in Washington and Alexandria, Virginia.*[8]

## The Philadelphia Mold

The Georgian rowhouse came to Baltimore via Philadelphia quite naturally. Baltimore's formative years were spent in a close relationship with Philadelphia. That older city set the standards and patterns for Baltimore to follow. Contact between the two cities was stimulated by natural similarities, direct transportation routes, and similar trade patterns. Businesses advertised in each others' newspapers, and builders ordered woodwork and window details from the same price books.[9] Philadelphia businessmen and artisans often found it advantageous to move to the rising young city to the south, just as aspiring Baltimore craftsmen sought their fortunes in the older city. And Baltimore patrons looked to Philadelphia craftsmen before Baltimore became a cultural center in its own right. It is logical, then, that Baltimore derived its rowhouse from the older city.

*18th century rowhouses in Baltimore bear the Philadelphia stamp, as the Captain Steele house at 931 Fell Street in Fells Point shows. Built between 1782 and 1796, its pitched roof with dormers, undecorated front, and well-balanced proportions were typical of the American Federal style in Baltimore, which was based on the British Georgian style.*

In the first quarter of the 19th century, there was in fact little discernible difference between the rowhouses of the two cities. The sobriety and moderation of the early Philadelphia rowhouse facades (owing, perhaps, to the city's founding by sober, moderate Quakers) characterized Baltimore's as well. The most obvious difference was the result of topography and the varying rhythms created by Baltimore's hills.

# The Creators of the Baltimore Aesthetic

Although Philadelphia provided Baltimore with the basic rowhouse type, outside architects, who came to Baltimore on special commissions, were the moderators of Baltimore's style. In pictures of 19th century Baltimore, there is a distinct architectural homogeneity which implies that local builders shared common ideas about design. This is apparent in most local buildings — public and private — from grand monuments to the ordinary rowhouse. Professional architects of national prominence who came to Baltimore in the early 19th century set the styles and standards that influenced local designers and eventually filtered into the common builders' vernacular. From that time on, Baltimore rarely generated change from within, but usually relied on outsiders for stylistic innovations.

Architects Benjamin Latrobe, Maximilian Godefroy, and Robert Mills, who played an important role in shaping the American Federal style, designed buildings in early 19th century Baltimore. Based on classical principles as the Georgian style was, the Federal style (generally given the dates of 1780 to 1820) resembled the preceding Georgian style. However, its combinations of geometric shapes, lack of ornament, and subtle rhythms of solids and voids, as well as its ampler proportions, made the Federal style clearer, simpler, and more forceful than its precursor. The Federal style represented America's break from Great Britain after the American Revolution.

With its roots in the classical tradition and its similarities with contemporaneous trends in British architecture, the Federal style appealed to the worldliness and cultural aspirations of America's merchant class. It was just right for Baltimore's temper at the beginning of the 19th century. Since Baltimore was not founded until 1729, it had not yet formed its own architectural traditions when Benjamin Latrobe and Maximilian Godefroy came to work in Baltimore seventy-five years later. For them, it was a "tabula rasa", a clean slate. Their principles became Baltimore's tradition.

The difference between Latrobe's, Mills', and Godefroy's influence in Baltimore and their influence in other cities was due to their presence at a critical time in Baltimore's development. Their style became indigenous here, and the Baltimore rowhouse retained its Federal countenance for a century. In other cities, such as Boston and Philadelphia, which had developed much earlier than Baltimore, the Federal style was one of a series of styles and soon gave way to the next trend.

The First Unitarian Church, designed by Maximilian Godefroy and built in 1818, and Benjamin Latrobe's Basilica of the Assumption built at the same time, represent the keynotes of the Federal style in Baltimore. The First Unitarian Church, whose form is composed of a cube surmounted by a hemisphere, and the Basilica, a group of interrelated rectangles with a hemispherical dome set on an octagonal drum, introduced a clarity of line and composition and an emphasis on form devoid of ornament that were the main themes of the Baltimore aesthetic.

While the dignity and elegant austerity of these two buildings were also attributes of the Baltimore rowhouse through the Victorian age, the connection between them is indirect. There is no evidence that Godefroy designed any rowhouses in Baltimore, and the evidence that Latrobe did is scanty. One source, however, credits Latrobe with four rowhouses on the east side of the 400 block of Park Avenue, the Swann Frick House on Franklin Street, and the Harper House on Cathedral Street, none of which is still standing.[10]

The Harper House and the Swann Frick House illustrate the classical composition which organized the facade like the parts of a classical column. This type, where the primary floor was the second story, was not used much in Baltimore. The similarity, however, between the clarity of Latrobe's rowhouse and Basilica facades and that of the typical Baltimore rowhouse of any period of the 19th century is obvious, and it is clear that Latrobe's buildings made a strong impact on the city.

For the first two decades of the 19th century, then, Latrobe's and Godefroy's influence was felt by cosmopolitan architects like Robert Mills, rather than local architects and builders. Gradually, however, the style filtered from the academic and nationally fashionable stratum into Baltimore's vernacular, as progressive local architects like Robert Cary Long, Sr. and George Millemon used it for major buildings such as the Peale Museum and the University of Maryland Medical School. Long and Millemon in turn passed the Federal style on to the more provincial rank of architects like William Small, who used it in his designs for rowhouses for the middle class.[11] These were im-

itated by builders who constructed rows of houses, and ultimately the Federal style became the hallmark of the average Baltimore rowhouse.

Latrobe did, in fact, design rowhouses in Philadelphia which set a precedent for Robert Mills, who worked with him from 1802 until 1809. When Mills went into practice on his own, he applied Latrobe's and Godefroy's new handling of forms to domestic architecture.[12] Like theirs, the work of the younger man was severe and plain, described later by Baltimoreans as "spartan". He worked in Baltimore between 1815 and 1829 and became one of the city's favorite architects.

Franklin Row built in Philadelphia in 1810 was Mills' attempt to create a row of houses as a unified architectural composition in the British tradition. It was one of the first attempts of an American-trained architect to do so and, as such, was a landmark in rowhouse design. Similar in design to Franklin Row, Mills' Waterloo Row on Calvert Street in Baltimore was a catalyst in the modernization of the city's rowhouse. It transposed Latrobe's principles to a smaller scale, one that influenced local architects in a way that Latrobe's Roman Catholic Cathedral could not.

Robert Cary Long, Sr., a Baltimore-born architect and contemporary of Latrobe, Godefroy, and Mills, was the next link in the chain from national to local style. He was apprenticed to a carpenter and learned from observation as well as pattern books. Since he did not learn the style formally, what he produced represents Baltimore's distillation of the Federal style. Long's choice of certain elements of Latrobe's, Godefroy's, and Mills' buildings to use in his own buildings represents the tailoring of a national fashion by a local designer to suit local tastes. The proportions, perfect symmetry, smooth, unbroken wall surfaces, and contrast of materials and colors on buildings like the Union Bank, the University of Maryland's School of Medicine, and his rowhouses on West Hamilton Street, linked Latrobe aesthetically with local builders. Because of their simplicity and restraint, Long's facades gave the impression of being classic without displaying any distinctly classical elements.

Other local architects like William Small modified the Federal style for the middle class and created what

*Maximilian Godefroy's First Unitarian Church, built between 1817 and 1818 and located at the corner of North Charles and West Franklin Streets, was an important milestone in the development of the Baltimore aesthetic. Its clarity of geometric forms and its reliance on the relationship between solids and voids for effect established a tradition that influenced the design of the vernacular rowhouse.*

*This row on West Hamilton Street, built in the early 19th century, is attributed to Robert Cary Long, Sr., a local architect. The large expanses of brick wall and marble accents were typical Baltimore features. The division of the facade and tripartite windows were seen earlier on Waterloo Row.*

*Attributed to Benjamin Latrobe, the Harper House, built between 1820 and 1840 and located on Cathedral Street where the Enoch Pratt Library now stands, shows the clarity and articulation of parts that became characteristic of the typical Baltimore rowhouse. The placement of the formal reception rooms on the "piano nobile", or second floor, was not favored by Baltimoreans, however.*

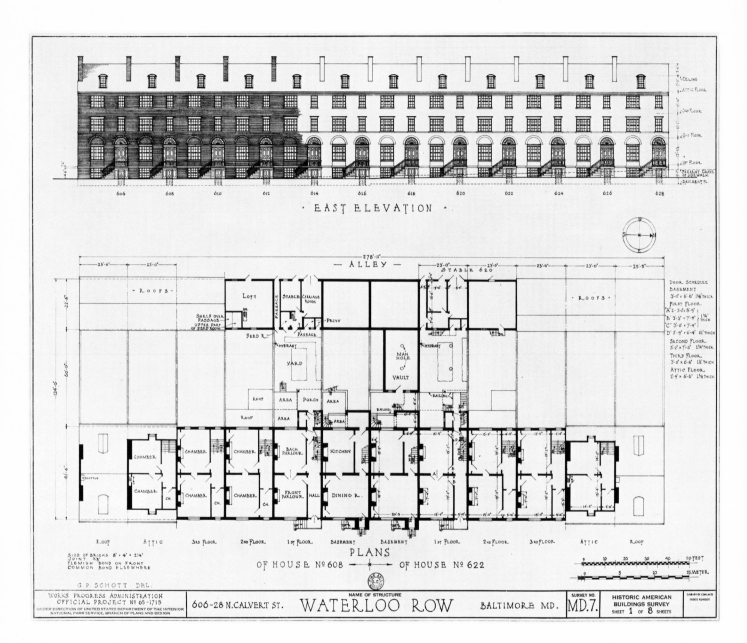

*Waterloo Row (demolished), designed in 1816 by Robert Mills and located on North Calvert Street between Centre and Monument, was one of Baltimore's first examples of a row designed as a unified architectural composition in the British tradition. The plan of the Waterloo Row houses, with a raised basement and reception rooms on the first floor, was preferred by Baltimoreans to the plan proposed by the Harper House (page 11). In this case, the dining room and kitchen are thought to have been located in the basement. The Waterloo Row facade translated the classical principles of Godefroy and Latrobe into a modest residential scale that local builders could understand. The graduated window proportions, blind tympana or arches, tripartite windows, and third floor windows suspended from the frieze, were features that became popular with local architects.*

was in many respects the archetypal Baltimore rowhouse. Small, who worked with Latrobe for two years between 1816 and 1818, was considered by architectural historian Robert F. Alexander to be "the most vigorous and effective local proponent of Latrobe's style.[13]" Architects who designed rowhouses before him worked primarily for wealthy merchants. But as industry replaced trade as Baltimore's leading commerce in the third decade of the 19th century, a strong middle class gained political control. With Small, the style of his predecessors was modified to become symbolic of the city's current political and social temper. It represented the position and aims of the social class that possessed, or aspired to possess, middle class respectability.

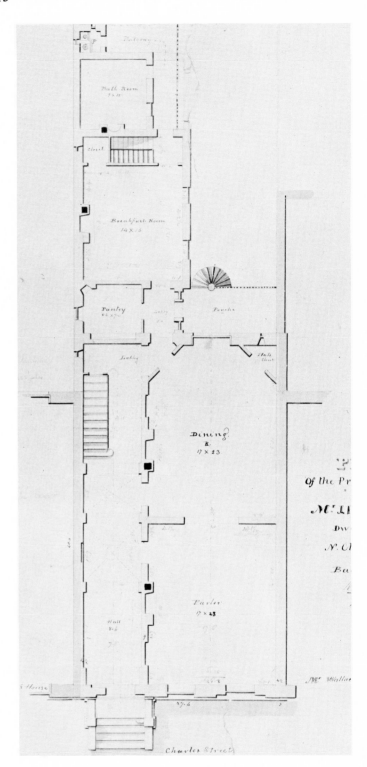

*The Joshua Cohen House (demolished), 415 North Charles Street, designed by William Small in 1830. The plain wall surface, clean-cut windows with stone sills, arched recesses with blind tympana, third floor windows suspended from the frieze, and graduated window proportions, perpetuated the tradition established by Robert Mills in Waterloo Row. Small's plans for the fourth floor indicate the presence of two front dormers, not drawn in the elevation, perhaps indicating a change in taste at this time.*

*Small's plan for the Joshua Cohen house was an elaboration of the basic Georgian rowhouse, with most of the service functions contained in a large rear wing. The house was four stories in height with a full basement.*

Small's style reflected his own craftsman's habits and practicality. His designs had none of the subtlety and little of the sophistication of Latrobe's designs. The bourgeois directness and simplicity of his buildings with their large proportions and generous spaces reflected the political transition from the sphere of the internationally-oriented merchant class to the mechanics, who were more limited culturally and inclined towards practical self-interests. Small's work embodied the virtues upheld by the middle class: directness, honesty, economy, practicality, and sobriety. And builders duplicated them literally by the dozen.

More than any architect, however, it was pattern books that popularized rowhouse designs. Speculative builders rarely employed architects, but built their rows using common sense, observation, and, most importantly, pattern books. John Hall — architect, cabinet-maker, draughtsman, and engraver — published three such books, two of which included house plans and exerted considerable influence on local builders.[14] Although no study has been made of the other American pattern books used in Baltimore, some of Hall's designs were influenced by the books of Minard Lafever. According to 18th century bookstore advertisements, foreign books that were sold in the city included *British Architect or the Builder's Treasury, The Practical Builder or Workman's General Assistant, The Town and Country Builder's Assistant,* Nicholson and Paine's *Carpenter,* Paine's *Practical Builder, Builder's Javel and Repository,* Crunden's *Designs,* Sheraton's *Ornaments,* Rawlin's *Designs,* and works by Batty Langley and William Pain.[15]

Builders were generally trained by apprenticeship, from pattern books, or occasionally, at a school like Cokesbury College in Abingdon, Harford County, Maryland. Since the rowhouse structure was so simple, small builders were capable of constructing the entire house. During the years of its huge population growth in the first quarter of the 19th century, Baltimore could not enforce apprenticeship laws, so craftsmen or laborers of almost any talent could find a market for their services. By 1810, there were almost fifty men calling themselves builders in the Baltimore directory, and there were many more house carpenters and masons who did the work of contractors. James Mosher, Surveyor of the Port from 1829 until 1840, worked on a number of important private houses in Baltimore and was the bricklayer on Robert Cary

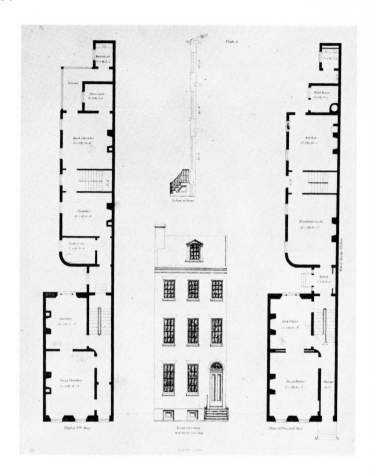

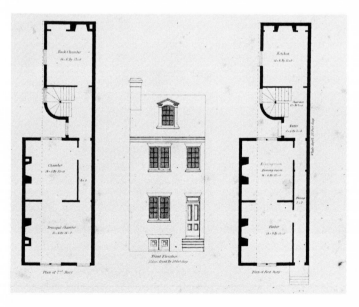

*John Hall's pattern book,* Modern Designs, *published in 1840, was an important influence on Baltimore builders. Hall offered a variety of plans although, as shown here, the same plan could be scaled up or down depending on the size of the house.*

Long's buildings. Other architect-builders who probably worked on rowhouses were John Scroggs, John Dalrymple, Christopher Deshon (who designed Pascault Row), Jacob Small, who worked with Mosher on the houses of John Hollins and James Buchanan on Washington Square, and William Steuart, a leading stonemason.

Many of the early immigrants were craftsmen educated either in formal European schools or by apprenticeship. Rowhouse details often revealed the background of the men who actually worked on the houses. The only craftsmen whose contributions have been documented were immigrants from Ireland. By the beginning of the American Revolution, Irish Catholic immigrants escaping persecution had landed in Baltimore by the thousands. Among these were architects like James Hogan, George M'Cutcheon, and Joseph Kennedy, who brought the great 18th century Irish tradition of decorative plasterwork to Baltimore.[16]

# Social, Economic, and Geographic Influences on the Baltimore Rowhouse

*Our generation in Baltimore owes much to the revolutionary generation of two centuries ago. They gave shape to the inner city, they provided the stuff for legend and local pride, and they sought and attained civic beauty. It could be said that they laid the foundations for the character of Baltimore upon which every generation, including ours, builds.*[17]

*— Wilbur Hunter.*

Arising out of the commercial necessity of providing a tobacco and wheat port for the hinterland, Baltimore was always intended to be a city. The rowhouse, the most urban of 18th century forms, thus gave Baltimore immediate metropolitan status. Annapolis, on the other hand, which served as the political and social capital for large landowners, had no need for rowhouses, and is still considered by many to be no more than a large town. Psychologically, the rowhouse was right for the burgeoning city of Baltimore.

Practically it was right, also: because the first settlers were discouraged by the hills surrounding Baltimore from spreading out into the countryside, they built close to the harbor where most of them were

employed. They soon found rowhouses to be the most efficient method of housing a large number of people in the small space. From the beginning, then, Baltimore was packed tightly, expanding row by row, rather than filling in a sparsely settled suburban area as most other cities did.

Even the wealthy merchants who had houses in the country needed houses in town near their source of income. Since space was limited, the rowhouse type was merely expanded to fit a higher income. Few cities besides Baltimore housed such a wide income range in rowhouses: they became what was essentially a democratic architectural type.

The difference between the houses for the rich and the houses for the poor was generally one of scale rather than form. One reason was the restraint the rich used in their townhouses, displaying their tastes for luxury in their country homes instead, as did the English. Townhouses, by comparison, were meant for comfort and convenience — functionalism prevailed. (The terms "rowhouse" and "townhouse" are generally interchangeable; here "townhouse" refers to those rowhouses that belonged to people who also had "country houses".) The fact that the men who lived in the more spacious and elegant rowhouses owned the land that workers' houses were built on may also account somewhat for the consistency of the form between classes. The simple serviceable elegance of the houses built for the upper classes was easily imitated in the smaller rowhouses. Even so, local historian Francis Beirne noted that townhouses "managed to present to the world an air of comfort, hospitality, and graciousness.[18]"

Poppleton's Plat, devised in 1812, was also partially responsible for the rowhouse character. Essentially a two-dimensional rather than a topographical survey, it gave inner city Baltimore its extraordinary character of straight rows of houses up and down hills. Furthermore, the 350-foot long blocks with service alleys that Poppleton laid out dictated a different kind of

*All that Baltimore aspired to architecturally were the most useful commercial buildings, the most comfortable houses, relatively modest municipal buildings, and the best of churches....a modest conservatism prevailed.*[19]

*— Spencer and Howland.*

*This section of Poppleton's Plat, laying out west-central Baltimore, shows the grid system that was responsible for the straight rows undulating over Baltimore's hills. Poppleton's hierarchy of street widths — front, side, and alley — also established the hierarchy of houses to be located on each type of street.*

rowhouse than New York's system of 200-foot long blocks without alleys. In New York's houses the service and basement entrances were in the front under the stoop. In Baltimore, they were in the rear, which was accessible by the alley or a tunnel between houses.

Poppleton's hierachy of street widths (front, side, and alley), perhaps more than house design, became a basic determinant of social strata in housing. Thomas Twining noted in 1894:

*The houses [on Market, now Baltimore, Street] were larger and handsomer in general than in the lower streets, but all were nearly upon the same plan, being built of red brick, having two or three windows in front, and three ranges of rooms or stories in height.*[20]

Neighborhoods were heterogeneous. Within them, there was class differentiation by elevation, street width, height and width of houses. But classes were generally not segregated by district or different types of houses.

Poppleton's plat also facilitated private speculative development. Baltimore's population was of a shrewd, mercantile nature. A British visitor in the early 19th century described the people as anxious "to get money,

honestly if they can, but at any rate to get it.[21]" The rapid growth of the city and huge daily influx of immigrants made land speculation one of the most lucrative investments for this property-conscious society. Indeed, historian Sherry Olson described the growth of Baltimore as:

*knotted in this web of mutual debts and transactions in land, the process of private development on credit, the expectation of ever-rising land values, and the dependence upon public investment decisions to generate land values. The city itself was to be the great speculation.*[22]

This financial climate, in which capital and hard currency were scarce and land was cheap, fostered a system of ground rents similar to London's. To give value to town lots or to make land produce income, a landowner rented his land to someone who had the capital to build on it. He in turn rented or sold the structures he built on the land. This device was beneficial to all involved. Both the landowner and the builder made money, and since the buyer did not have to purchase the ground, the cost to him was often 20% less than if the houses had been built by the usual system. A row of six 2½-story houses is said to have

*The 300 block of North Carrollton Street in West Baltimore, built in the mid- to late-19th century. Houses on narrow side streets were generally small-scale versions of houses on broad front streets. Thus, the Carrollton Street rowhouses look much like their Bolton Street peers (page 17). Both rows are set on a raised base and have planar facades with sharply-incised openings, the whole composition crowned by an ornamented projecting cornice. The white wooden steps were the inexpensive version of white marble.*

17

*A century after Kennington Road in London (page 6) and the Captain Steele House in Baltimore (page 9), the Georgian origins of Baltimore's rowhouses were still apparent. The 1400 block of Bolton Street in Bolton Hill, built around 1867, still fits Nicholas Pevsner's description of the Georgian style, which he called: "a universally valid one, a neutral style as it were. Windows were cut into the walls without any molding. Roofs were hardly visible from below. Little was demanded of differentiation. Beauty or its opposite was the result of fitnesses of proportion, the relation of wall and void.[23]" The marble base, flattened roof, ornamented cornice and doorway, and attenuated proportions, were elements that transformed the typical Georgian London terrace house into the typical Baltimore rowhouse.*

cost one builder $400 apiece to build, and he sold them for $450-475 apiece. He retained ownership of the land, charging ground rent of $11 a year.[24] (Some ground rents ran as high as $50 per year.) Thus, the builder made little construction profit, but rather a long-term investment gain. Rowhouses were found to be a fast and cheap way to exploit land as well as an impetus to homeownership, since the selling price was substantially lower than in other cities without the ground rent system.

Letitia Stockett suggested another reason for the popularity of the system:

*A man who buys title to land in fee simple owns real estate, and his wife's signature is necessary if he wishes to sell the land. On the other hand, a perpetual lease makes the land personal property, and a wife's signature is not needed for the disposition.[25]*

The system of building and loan associations continued to encourage homeownership in the second half of the century. By allowing members to buy houses with as little as one-fifth of the purchase price, building and loan associations brought homeownership within almost everyone's reach. A *Sunpapers* article (November 9, 1894) extolled the virtues of rowhouses for this reason:

*Small houses. In a walk over our city one is struck with a feature which so far as our observation of large cities extends, characterizes Baltimore alone — certainly to a greater degree than any other, viz: its numerous, small, neat and comfortable dwellings, adapted to the means of individuals of nearly every circumstance in life. Some portions of the city are ornamented...with fine and handsome rows of such buildings, and the bright door brasses, the clean steps and well-washed windows — in short, the general air of neatness and comfort which characterizes them all, indicate that peace, happiness, content and similar virtues are their tenants.*

Rowhouses, which for Baltimore were synonymous with homeownership, appealed to the conservative middle class ideals of Baltimore's population. Four-story brick tenements built on Parkin Street by Ross Winans were a resounding financial failure. Gerald W. Johnson blamed the paucity of local cultural activity on the fact that citizens were tied to their homes like medieval serfs. To them "eluding foreclosure was far more important than pursuing culture.[26]" According to Sherry Olson, redevelopment was discouraged as confusion over land titles arose when ground rents were divided among heirs. Also, as buildings depreciated, the fixed charge seemed disproportionately great.[27] The system that initially had encouraged development served to restrain re-building activity, so Baltimore retained much of its early countenance.

Housing gradually became a manifestation of Baltimore's innate conservatism. Local architect J.B. Noel Wyatt wrote in 1895, "as [the ground rent system] exists in Baltimore at present and in long past, it is evidently a great hindrance...to a free growth of good architecture on a large scale.[28]" For landowners it was a tax-free and low-risk investment. If a houseowner failed to pay the ground rent, the owner could reclaim the ground and the house. Thus, because they were responsible to landowners for their investment, builders were checked from building anything shoddy or faddish, and instead constructed houses of enduring quality and aesthetic appeal. Furthermore, a clientele of homeowners had a different criterion for houses than renters because a house had to be a good long-term investment. High standards of building for all classes and a design that rarely varied became the hallmarks of Baltimore rowhouses.

Local resources of building materials also placed certain constraints on rowhouse design. There was an abundance of good clay in the region, and Baltimore's bricks early on gained such a reputation for quality that they were sometimes exported to other cities. Benjamin Latrobe planned to use Baltimore bricks for at least one of his projects in Philadelphia. And F. Scott Fitzgerald found the color of the bricks exceptional, likening them to "an old opera cloak of his mother's that was full of tints yet was of no tint — a mere reflector of light.[29]"

The marble quarries, however, supplied the panache to Baltimore's design. The white marble relieved the monotony of the solid red walls, and the combination of the two gave Baltimoreans what they wanted — solid respectability with a touch of elegance, or, as one native noted, "brick gave the city's houses strength, but marble gave them stature.[30]"

Marble came into general use in Baltimore in 1815 with the construction of the Washington Monument. In 1827, Anthony Trollope's mother visited Baltimore and commented on the "abundance of white marble" decorating the houses.[31] By 1847, thirteen Baltimore quarries were producing marble as a building stone. As the marble was nearby, cheap, and of high quality, it was used for the trim and steps of most rowhouses. If builders could not afford marble, they tried to obtain the same genteel effect by painting wooden steps white.

Brick and marble suited the smooth, elegant facades of the Federal style well. In Boston and Philadelphia, where it was hard to obtain, brick was established as the aristocratic material and most Federal buildings were of brick. The abundance of brick in Baltimore made it practical for all buildings, even after the mid-

dle of the 19th century when the use of brick had become unfashionable in Philadelphia. In the Victorian period when New York propagated its brownstones up and down the coast and into midwestern cities, Baltimore built only a few. Since the stone was not available locally, it was not financially feasible to switch to another material. Brick and marble had become Baltimore's idiom.

Whether Baltimore embraced the Federal style with the intent of making it its own, or whether Baltimore did not have the imagination to develop a new style is a rhetorical issue. It is clear, however, that Baltimore's financial system, local building supplies, and the demand for a certain kind of housing checked radical deviations from the standard form. Also, because builders rather than architects constructed the rows, they were more likely to continue in a familiar mode and one they knew would sell. The traditional Federal rowhouse was a sure sell and builders had little incentive to try new styles.

# The Aesthetic of Baltimore's Temperament

Why didn't popular taste demand a new design? Why were Baltimoreans content with the old-fashioned Federal style for so long, while other cities welcomed new fashions enthusiastically? The answer lies in the temperament of the city.

Baltimore had always possessed what John Dorsey and James Dilts describe as "a quiet and smug inhibition[32]": smug because it assumes that whatever it has or does is the best and needs no change; inhibited because of its innate fear of being vulgar. Baltimoreans take inverse pride in not being noticed (which, some say, comes from not being noticed in the first place). Their houses, Dilts and Dorsey continue, "seem to project not only what they are, but also, as a virtue, the quality of not being something more." Thus the modest refinement of the Federal style suited Baltimore's self-image.

Baltimore did not readily accept new styles, as that might be construed as "showy". J.B. Noel Wyatt wrote of the city's "sense of discretion and fitness [that] hesitated the thrust of the new and doubtful innovation[s].[33]" Letitia Stockett pronounced, "Baltimore will not suffer change unless compelled by an act of Providence.³⁴" One reason Baltimore lagged behind other eastern cities by the middle of the 19th century after its auspicious start was that it did not really enjoy being in the mainstream. It never tried to start and rarely followed trends. By always remaining second in stylishness to Boston, Philadelphia, or New York, Baltimore retained more of its original character than other cities.

Indeed, the rowhouses are a product and a visible manifestation of Baltimore's personality. Perhaps the most obvious attribute of the Baltimore rowhouse is its state of "non". It is not garish or overbearing, nor is it without distinction. It is neither stylish nor unstylish; it isn't too meager for the rich nor too lavish for the poor. Its character comes from its negative characteristics: its lack of ornament and of pretension, its plainness, its austerity. As H.L. Mencken wrote:

*The two-story houses that were put up in my boyhood forty years ago, all had a kind of unity, and many of them were far from unbeautiful... The builders of the time were not given to useless ornamentation: their houses were plain in design and restful to the eye. A long row of them, to be sure, was somewhat monotonous, but it at least escaped being trashy and annoying. Before every row, in those days, ranged a file of shade-trees. The green against the red, with flecks of white showing through, was always dignified and sometimes very charming.*³⁵

A comparison with the New York rowhouse clarifies what makes Baltimore's unique. Throughout the 19th century, New York's houses outdid those of other cities in size and splendor. Social life was more competitive than elsewhere and the home often symbolized a family's status and wealth. In Baltimore, however, class was denoted by restraint. Baltimore's upper classes found ostentation, particularly on the exterior, anathema.

In New York, city houses were much more formal, ornate, and fashionable than suburban or country houses. Baltimore's gentry, on the other hand, lavished their wealth on country homes. Ease and convenience were Baltimore's urban and New York's suburban priorities. Montgomery Schuyler wrote in 1899 of the originality and fantasy of the New York small house, compared with the "Quakerish simplicity" of Philadelphia and the "Puritanic bleakness" of Boston.³⁶ New York was quick to pick up on, and lead, trends. Its rowhouse changed identities with great fickleness and flourish. In Baltimore, any change in style occurred long after New York had advertised it (at least a generation later) and on a much more modest scale. Baltimore acknowledged styles with a nod—a fashionable new cornice or doorway— but the essential form remained serenely the same.

*This pair of houses at 626 and 628 Shakespeare Street in Fells Point is typical of cottages built for artisans and craftsmen at the end of the 18th century.*

# Part Two

# The Development of the Baltimore Rowhouse

## The Evolution of the Baltimore Rowhouse: 1780 - 1820

We have defined the general guidelines for the design of "those old placid rows." The next step is to trace the evolution of the design.

Until the end of the 18th century, nearly all dwellings were two stories, with peaked shingled roofs and chimneys on the houses, kitchens, and back buildings. The first brick house was built in 1735, and by the end of the century, Baltimore was producing its own brick in huge quantities.[37] Because of frequent fires, a city ordinance was enacted in 1799 to prohibit the erection of wooden buildings in the city. The character of the Baltimore rowhouse owes much both to the cheapness of brick and to this ordinance.

In the late 18th century, wealthy citizens usually lived in townhouses, which made the same economical use of land as rowhouses. Compared to the merchant's townhouses, rowhouses for artisans were modest two-room dwellings. Speculative builders often constructed the houses in pairs, one to rent out and one to live in themselves. Rowhouses saved builders as much as 25% of the cost of individual houses because only the front and back required the full strength and finish, and more houses could fit on the lot than if built separately. Tenants saved on heating and upkeep as there were only two walls they could call their own.

The accumulation of wealth in the early 19th century made rowhouse construction possible on a larger scale. Wealthy merchants found "ranges" to be a good investment and built rows of six or twelve: Pascault's houses on Lexington Street, William Patterson's Wharf, William Shipley's row on Pratt Street, Wales and Clopper's on Bowley's Wharf, an "elegant four-story row" on St. Paul Street, and others on George and Sharpe Streets.[38] As Baltimore's growth rate soared, and with it the demand for living space, rows eight to twenty houses long were built by speculators. One visitor to Federal Baltimore noted that, on the whole, blocks generally consisted of adjoining houses interspersed with identical units, making the streets of Baltimore "nearly all of the same appearance.[39]"

By the first quarter of the 19th century, these houses usually consisted of two rooms per floor: reception rooms on the ground floor, one or two floors of bedrooms, and an attic for servants. Earlier houses may not have had back buildings, or only a back kitchen with a tall chimney.[40] Others had the kitchen and dining room in the basement, although this was generally later than the plan with the separate kitchen. To get light into the basement, the first story was raised above the sidewalk, so the entrance was approached by several steps. A "commodious and elegant" three-story house, advertised for sale in 1800, contained on the ground floor "an entry, parlor, dining and housekeeper's room which by a piazza and pantry communicates with a spacious back kitchen"; on the second floor, "a saloon (sic) with two fireplaces occupying the whole front of the house (34 feet in the clear).[41]" When this room stretched across the full width of the house in the front, it was found to be particularly suitable for entertaining.

As the sophistication of rowhouses increased to match the townhouse design, the form became democratized and the two types merged. The difference in the class of houses became, "with conspicuous exceptions", as local architect J.B. Noel Wyatt wrote in 1895, one of "degree rather than kind. The more pretentious and expensive were simply larger, in number rather than size of rooms and richer details of interior finish.[42]" In other cities, New York and Boston for example, houses for the rich became more distinct beginning with the Greek Revival period as new styles demanded ornament that only they could afford. There, only the most modest houses retained the plain Federal style during subsequent years.

At the beginning of the 19th century, however, the homogeneity of Baltimore's rowhouses was typical of most cities. This was due in part to the nature of the Federal style itself. The emphasis on proportions and form, the simple ornament, and modest size were Federal dicta in all cities. The control inherent in the style allowed little improvisation. Even in New York, houses of this period were brick, with door and window trim of marble, brownstone, or granite—modestly detailed and discreetly two-dimensional. At this point the Federal style was not peculiar to Baltimore.

But it lingered there because an innate conservatism prevailed. The rich did not try to keep pace with other cities, and by about 1830 the same rowhouse type accommodated all classes. Builders imitated the larger, grander houses, so the same elements recurred down through the ranks of rowhouses. The minimal design was easily adopted by builders who had tight budgets. In general, changes of style on the fine rowhouses were picked up by builders, although usually at least ten years later.

The modesty of the fronts often belied the luxury

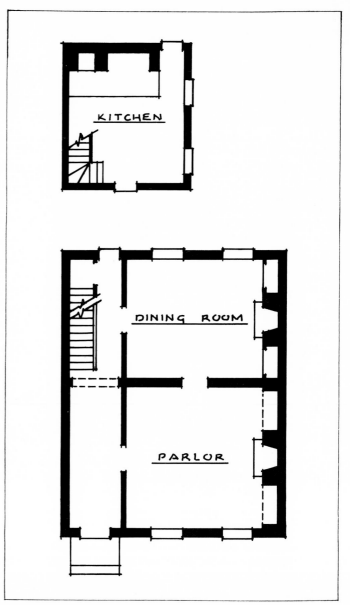

*Until alleys were laid out by Poppleton's Plat in 1822, access to back buildings and yards was through arched tunnels between houses, as on Stirling Street.*

*The plan of 802 South Ann Street, constructed in 1796, was the archetypal plan for rowhouses built in the late 18th century and was commonly used until the middle of the 19th century. In comparison to the grander 1621 Thames Street, it is only three bays wide and almost ten feet narrower, with the kitchen housed in a separate rear building. By the beginning of the 19th century, however, a pantry connected the kitchen to the house. Another contemporary variation on this plan placed the kitchen in the rear room of the basement and the staircase in a rear projection, without a side hall, which allowed the rooms greater width. Houses of this genre generally had staircases with mahogany or walnut handrails and painted rectangular balusters. Mantels were usually of wood.[43]*

and individuality of the interiors. Baltimoreans spoke proudly of the "many magnificent private houses, which furnish at once, proofs of the distinguished taste and opulence of their owners.[44]" Lest this seem contradictory to Baltimore's characteristic reserve, it must be noted that it was typical of Baltimoreans not to make much effort to impress outsiders—by distinctive facades, for example. They usually revealed their personalities only to those they chose to invite *into* their homes. Interior decoration and furniture gave each house the individuality that the plans and elevations did not.

Interiors were often influenced by the latest taste or foreign trends and more than made up for the lack of ornament on the exterior. The finest imported decorations graced Baltimore's houses, although local craftsmen were soon competing with their own products in the latest and most elegant mode. Some rooms were whitewashed or painted, others were ornamented with figured borders or patterned wallpapers. Most of Baltimore's wallpaper was imported from London, Liverpool, Marseilles, Germany, the East Indies, Boston, or Philadelphia. By 1801, however, Baltimore had two of its own manufactors: Thomas and Caldcleugh and Abraham R. Williams. Wallpaper was considered appropriate for every room in the house, and rented houses were advertised as "handsomely furnished, and papered up to the garret." Wallpainting to imitate marble, panelling, or wallpaper was also popular and according to a house painter, William Priest, healthier than wallpaper itself: "Paper hangings in a warm climate are a receptacle for contagious infection, and a harbor for dust and vermin." Rural scenes, landscapes, or floral motifs decorated overmantels or panels between the mantel shelf and ceiling. Bands of solid color or decorated with festoons and other motifs were painted or stenciled at the tops of walls, around windows or doors, or at the chair-rail level.[45]

Intricate stucco or composition work often adorned fireplaces, cornices, ceilings, doors, and windows. Local artisans either applied precast pieces or molded the stucco directly on the surface to be decorated. Irish craftsmen may have been responsible for Baltimore's best plasterwork, which displayed the kind of naturalistic details popularized by 18th century British architect, Robert Adam. Favored motifs were festoons, urns, paired human figures, and trophies of crossed torches and quivers. One 1797 advertisement offered molded plaster "landscape tablets, vases, rich flower festoons, wheat, vine, and ivy, eagles, Apollo and Lyre.[46]" Sometimes the same design was repeated on the chimney piece, the door entablature, panels below the recessed window, and the niches flanking the fireplace.

Wooden mantels were usually decorated with composition work or a combination of composition and carved designs. Wealthier houses may have had imported marble mantels or fireplaces decorated with imported tiles. The mantelpiece was supported by columns or pilasters, and elliptical engaged columns held the overmantel arch. The hallway arch, which separated the entrance hall from the stair hall, was similarly supported and was sometimes embellished with a keystone and carved motifs like fluting and pearls on its back, front, or underside.

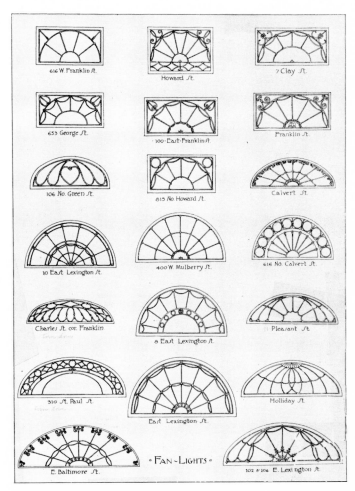

*Fanlights used on Baltimore's Federal rowhouses, as measured and drawn by W. Alexander in 1898.*

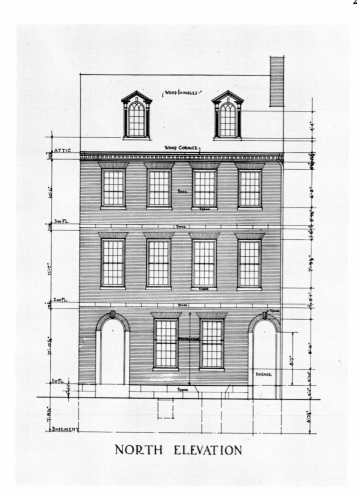

NORTH ELEVATION

*Typical of houses built at the end of the 18th century for wealthy merchants, 1621 Thames Street (ca. 1790) was set on a low stone foundation and was four bays (34' 6") wide and 3½ stories high plus basement. The fourth bay on the ground story accomodated an arched service passage to the yard. The basement contained the kitchen and service rooms, the first floor had the reception rooms, the main drawing room and bedrooms were on the second floor, and more bedrooms were on the third and fourth floors. First floor rooms were 12' 0" in height; second floor rooms were 11' 7"; third floor rooms 10' 6". The back building and connecting link may have been added later, since houses of this period more typically had separate back buildings. Interior ornament was extensive: plaster cornices in the larger rooms, wooden shutters, moldings, and chair-rails, arches flanking the parlor fireplace, and cupboards with butterfly shelves flanking the dining room fireplace. The graceful Adam style composition work on the door entablature was typical ornament for houses of this size.*[47]

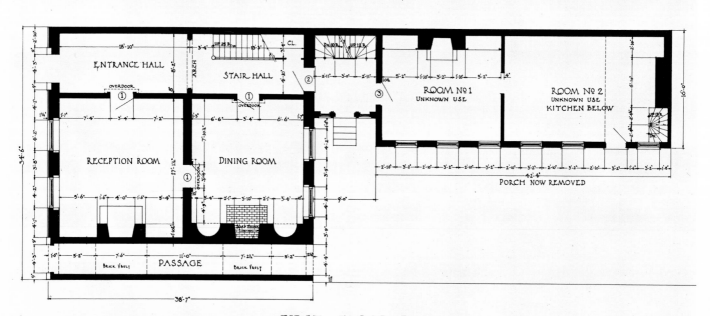

FIRST FLOOR PLAN

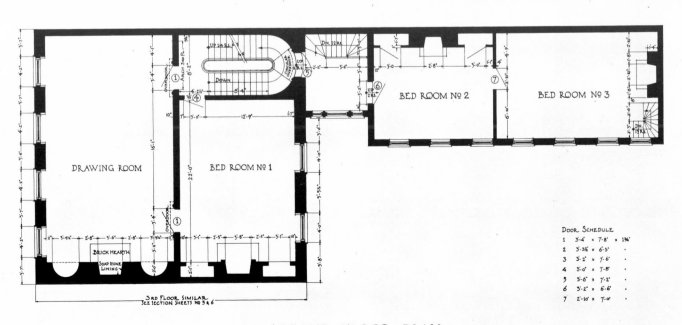

DOOR SCHEDULE
1   3'-4"  × 7'-8"  × 1¾"
2   3'-3½" × 6'-5"   "
3   3'-2"  × 7'-6'   "
4   3'-0"  × 7'-8'   "
5   3'-6"  × 7'-2'   "
6   3'-2"  × 6'-6'   "
7   2'-10' × 7'-0'   "

SECOND FLOOR PLAN

*Pascault Row (Federal style), 1816, West Lexington Street.*

# The Greek Revival Style: 1820-1845

It is always difficult to date Baltimore houses since they did not take up styles casually and were hesitant to relinquish them. The Greek Revival style seems to have appeared in the finest houses around 1820 and continued through the 1840's. It lasted at least another ten years on smaller rowhouses. By this time, the Baltimore rowhouse had begun to develop in a different direction from Philadelphia's rowhouse. With the Greek Revival style, the houses of the younger city took on their own character with confidence and skill.

In the finer houses a stylistic as well as proportional change was taking place. As a reaction to what J.B. Noel Wyatt called the "somewhat 'ad libitum' and at-

tenuated use of colonial details[48]", the 1830's in Baltimore witnessed more strictly classical and monumental proportions. This is the period when the rowhouse felt the influence of Latrobe, Mills, and Godefroy. The tradition of broad facades of brick with simply-treated and well-disposed window openings continued, now crowned by a classical cornice. The chief ornamental feature was a Doric or Ionic portico, usually projecting. On a more modest scale, the portico was suggested by rectangular pilasters set flat against the facade and supporting a horizontal entablature or sometimes a triangular pediment. The portico suited Baltimore's peculiar sense of fitness, conveying grandeur without self-consciousness. Wyatt described it as "of just such degree of monumental dignity as may fittingly belong to private residences,

*Greek Revival rowhouses formerly on Cathedral Street. J. B. Noel Wyatt praised Baltimore's Greek Revival rowhouses: "So good are these bits of Greek reproduction in Baltimore that their merits seldom fail to attract the attention of architectural connoisseurs from other cities, and, indeed, we do not know of anything quite so good of the kind and of that perfection in New York, Philadelphia, or Boston.[49]" In this period, Baltimore's rowhouses began to develop an aesthetic distinctive from that of any other city; their proportions became attenuated as they were placed on a marble base, and they were given a Greek entrance portico and a cornice of increasing definition. The division of the facade into base, shaft, and capital was a variation on the Georgian "piano nobile" theme.*

without being sufficiently obtrusive to suggest a public building.[50]"

Except for the portico, the Greek Revival style closely resembled the Federal style. The psychological motivation, however, was very different: the Classical ideal of forms as beautiful in themselves changed to the Romantic concept of forms as symbols that evoked particular associations. Like the Federal style, the Greek Revival style still advocated the red brick wall set off by white marble trim. But it sought greater dignity and monumentality. Ceilings were higher and windows longer, creating a taller and more impressive house, which now often had a full third floor instead of a pitched roof with dormer windows.

An awareness of the importance of the streetscape and the unity of the street front, first suggested in Robert Mills' Waterloo Row constructed in 1819, was sharpened. Forms and ornament were simplified: the massive scale and elemental shapes of the Doric portico illustrate this. The one, two, or three-panelled door replaced the more elaborate six-panelled Federal door, while the leaded fanlight gave way to a simpler rec-

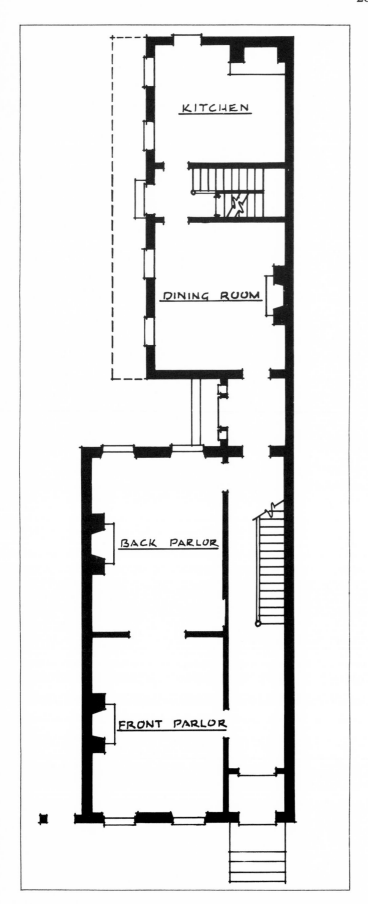

*By 1820, the rear wing or "back building" increased in size and the number of services it housed. Now two or three stories tall like these in the Otterbein area, it grew to almost the length of the main house, containing service facilities like heaters for water, bathrooms, the laundry room, kitchen, and storage rooms, as well as the family dining room (breakfast room), and bedrooms. The Joshua Cohen House (page 13) placed the nursery and "meat house" on the second floor and the servants' chambers on the third floor of the back building. On upper floors, back rooms remained a stair landing lower than the front rooms.*

*In this plan of a typical Greek Revival rowhouse, 714 Park Avenue, constructed around 1835, the entrance hall was replaced by a shallow vestibule, and the two first floor rooms became a double parlor separated by sliding doors or columns. This feature may have been introduced by Robert Mills in his plan for Waterloo Row in 1816 (page 12). The back parlor was sometimes used as a formal dining room, although the back building had developed to accomodate both the kitchen and family dining room or breakfast room. A narrow passage with a side entrance usually connected the two sections. The Waterloo Row parlor (frontispiece) illustrates the simplification and classicization of forms that took place in the Greek Revival period. Parlor mantels were often marble with free-standing columns or pilasters, while dining room mantels were generally of wood. Mahogany, or wood painted to look like mahogany, was popular for doors. Staircase balusters were usually painted and of a round, tapered shape.* [50a]

*Greek Revival ironwork usually consisted of geometric shapes.*

tangular transom. Bricks, formerly laid in Flemish bond which alternated the ends and sides of brick in a dot-dash-dot pattern, were now laid with their sides continuous in a common bond pattern.

The interiors showed an increased grandeur as well. Architectural historian Talbot Hamlin commented that "almost nowhere else is the complete break with the richness of Federal-style details so apparent as in Baltimore.[51]" Forms were simplified and strengthened. The airy delicacy of the Adam style applied decoration was replaced by classical forms that depended on shape rather than surface ornament for their character. As on the exterior, where the doorway had become the focus of the facade, there was a focusing of interest here too. Instead of embellishing several elements (fireplace, door and window architraves, overmantel arch) as the Federal style did, ornament was simplified and consolidated. Only one or two elements were accented: for example a ceiling modillion or a pair of columns dividing the double drawing room.

Ironwork was one way to adorn a building without being excessive. It had decorated London terraces since the 18th century, but did not appear to a significant extent in Baltimore until the period of the Greek Revival style. Krug and Son, founded in the 1820's, the Bartlett Hayward Company, an iron stove factory founded in 1837, and Pine and Company, founded in 1849, made Baltimore a center for manufacturing wrought and cast iron, and for exporting it in large quantities to other American cities.

Typically, Greek Revival ironwork was chaste. It appeared as balustrades on parlor windows, as railings along steps or to separate deep areaways and basement stairs from the sidewalk. The door covering the coal shute was often decorated as well, and cellar window gratings were frequently of wrought iron. The patterns advertised by local manufacturers like Hayward, Bartlett, and Company resemble those advertised for sale by New York merchants at that time, generally consisting of simple patterns of geometric shapes: rectangles, diamonds, and ovals.[52]

Meanwhile, the population growth of the 1840's and 1850's was so great that speculative building of blocks of rowhouses "got underway with a vengeance.[53]" These rows, like their finer counterparts, also exhibited classical elements. John Hall's pattern books, published in 1840 and 1848, are a realistic index to the general stylistic consciousness of Baltimore builders at this time. Not only did his books exercise considerable influence on local builders, but they are also a synthesis of designs that had already appeared in Baltimore and Philadelphia rowhouses.[54] Hall included only examples of classical character—an illustration of the ubiquity of the Greek Revival style.

The Greek Revival style ultimately reaffirmed Baltimore's austere tendencies and its instincts that beauty lay in forms rather than ornament. The planar, subtle facade, spaciousness, and the use of single details to accent forms and proportions became typical of its rowhouses until the end of the 19th century.

# The Italianate Style: 1845-1870

"Nothing denotes more greatly a nation's advancement in civilization than the ornate and improved styles of its architecture, and the erection of palatial private residences,[55]" declared one magazine article heralding the Italianate style. The style's bold forms, elaborate ornament, sumptuous elegance, and monumental streetscape constituted an exuberant response to industrialization. Based on Italian Renaissance palazzos, this mode first appeared in London in 1829 on the Travelers' Club, designed by Sir Charles Barry. Arthur Gilman's article about palazzos in the *North American Review,* published in 1844, and the Philadelphia "Atheneum", designed by John Notman and built between 1845 and 1847, were catalysts in the development of the Italianate style in America.[56]

*Until approximately 1840, the common vernacular rowhouse, like the Edgar Allan Poe house on Amity Street, was still set low to the sidewalk and had a gable roof with dormer. (Upper left.)*

*By 1840, the roof gable was beginning to widen, and a full third floor with small horizontal windows replaced the dormers, as these Otterbein houses illustrate. (Upper right.)*

*Around the middle of the 19th century, the third floor windows became full-size, as the proportions grew attenuated, a development that had occurred earlier on the larger rowhouses and brought the two classes of houses into relative congruence. Typically, windows had flat-arched brick lintels, and facades were laid in common bond, a pattern composed of rows of stretchers, or bricks with their sides facing out, sometimes alternating with rows of headers, or bricks whose ends are exposed. (Lower left.)*

*These houses in the 200 block of North Carey Street near Franklin Square nominally belonged to the French Second Empire style. Even the mansard roofs and ornamental porticos, however, did not disguise the typical Baltimore rowhouse.*

In Baltimore, the first signs were early: the flat-roofed presbytery of St. Peter's Church, designed by Robert Cary Long, Jr. in 1843, signalled the introduction of the Italianate mode to the city.[57] Baltimore's response to the style was enthusiastic but, compared with other cities, inhibited. The Italianate mode suited Baltimore's position at the time: it had finally achieved genuine metropolitan proportions. Baltimore's first comprehensive water system, public rapid transit system, and public parks were introduced; the city raised its first city hall; and Enoch Pratt, George Peabody, and Johns Hopkins gave Baltimore its first great philanthropic institutions.

This new stature was reflected in the rowhouse built at this time. A row of eight mansions built by Col. John Gittings illustrates the elaboration of the rowhouse around the middle of the century. They each had flues of Maryland soapstone and mantels of Italian marble, speaking tubes and bells in every room, and gas light throughout. Each house was twenty-four feet wide, with a back building as long as the main structure—forty-eight feet. Yet the houses, according to one observer, were "still of chaste design." A row on Madison Street had patent force pumps, a hot water system, a "bathing house", bells, and a central furnace.[58]

Just as brick passed out of fashion in Philadelphia and New York, Baltimore also renounced it—briefly. Brownstone was imported from quarries in New York, New Jersey, and the Connecticut Valley. Its light weight and ease of handling offset the cost of transporting it south, so it was popular at the outset of the Italianate style. In addition to the brownstone houses built on Mt. Vernon Place, Canby Place, and Jackson Square, other rows like Waverly Terrace (built by speculators from Wilmington) of uncharacteristic style and splendor were also appearing. A new prosperity made some Baltimoreans crave a domestic grandeur that the indigenous rowhouse did not offer.

Overall, however, Baltimore maintained the status quo. The Italianate style represented a radical deviation from the Baltimore aesthetic. Rich ornamental facades had little in common with the severe planarity of Baltimore's rows. Therefore, the city treated the Italianate style as it had the Greek Revival style. It incorporated certain Italianate elements into its rows without changing their essential character.

With the exception of a few brownstone incursions, Baltimore continued to use brick, although by this time New York used brick for only its most modest rows. Baltimore adopted the flat Italianate roof easily, due in part to the fire ordinance of 1834. This required parapet walls extending above the roof line and roofs that sloped back towards the alleys. The reach of fire ladders set height restrictions and encouraged the practice of the lighted basement, a half-story below ground. New houses were built without peaked roofs and dormer windows, and older houses were reconstructed by raising the roof line to the new standard.[59]

Proportions were attenuated. Buildings became taller, "their magnificence emphasized by their magnified height."[60] Windows lengthened and widened: at the parlor level they were floor length, and with each successive floor they diminished in height—a system that emphasized the verticality of the facade.

Italianate decoration accented certain aspects of the Baltimore facade. Cornices, advocated by mid-19th century architect A.J. Downing as "one of the simplest, cheapest, and most effective modes of giving force and spirit to any building,[61]" became more assertive. They projected farther than earlier cornices and were usually supported on consoles underlined by single rows of dentilling. Downing noted that this type of cornice could add "picturesque richness" to houses by casting deep shadows over the surface, and that it set "good" proportions by limiting the distance the eye could travel up the facade.

Doorways were thought by one magazine journalist of the time to be "the most indispensable feature of the structure, and therefore calls loudly for adornment, and should generally be distinguished by more impressive decoration than any other feature.[62]" Baltimore replaced the Doric portico with a projecting rounded or rectangular door frame that either surrounded the whole doorway or was supported on unornamented brackets or consoles. Thus decorated, the doorway and vestibule became the dramatic focal point of the facade.

Windows were also adorned. By the 1840's window lintels, previously of stone, marble, wood, or brick laid in flat or segmental arches, were sometimes of iron painted to resemble stone. Two of the most popular patterns for lintels were a Greek Revival form with an anthemion motif in the center, and a heavy composition of dentils and an anthemion. In the 1850's, elaborate projecting iron hood cornices were used occasionally. The shadows they cast on facades suited Italianate taste, but hood cornices enjoyed only brief popularity in Baltimore. A more modest version, "basket handle" arches, were no more endearing. They obscured the proportions and coherence of the rowhouse facade, which was not to Baltimoreans' liking.

More attractive to Baltimoreans were cast iron railings, balustrades, first floor window boxes, and upper story window gratings. Although heavier and coarser than the preceding wrought iron ornament, the patterns were relatively delicate compared to New York's. Elegant cast iron porches on the backs or sides of cor-

*Although neither their style nor their splendor was typical of Baltimore, Waverly Terrace, built in 1850 by speculators from Wilmington, Delaware, illustrates Baltimore's enthusiastic response to industrialization. This row is located on Franklin Square in West Baltimore.*

ner houses were also a feature of this era. A four-story house on the corner of Centre Street and Washington Place was one of the first to have an iron verandah in the 1850's.[63]

To be sure, cast iron suited rowhouse speculators admirably, since, as noted by a *Sunpapers* article in 1847, "when painted, [it] will appear as well as the most costly stone or marble work, while the expense is not much more, if as much, as if constructed of the more perishable material—wood.[64]" Iron was cheap to produce, yet as marble had done earlier, added that touch of panache to the minimal rowhouse to give it sales appeal.

Still, rowhouses maintained their strait-laced two-dimensionality—with a few Italianate embellishments, to be sure, but these were purely cosmetic. Adopted in this way, the Italianate style was very popular in Baltimore. Most new houses were built and old houses remodelled in this manner. David Carson proposed the addition of a brownstone cornice, window trim, balcony, and entrance to his simple red brick facade. The "veritable fever [that] arose of building rows of houses by the mile," noted by local architect George Frederick in the 1850's, spread the style over the city.[65] With its projecting cornices, door frames, steps, and occasional window lintels and sills, the Italianate style

*More typically, rows of this period, like this one on Union Square where H. L. Mencken lived, adopted the Italianate style with greater restraint. Facade proportions became more elegant and attenuated, while they gained ornate projecting cornices and door frames. It was surely rows like this one that prompted Henry James to describe Baltimore's houses as "quiet old ladies seated, with their toes tucked-up on uniform footstools, under the shaded candlesticks of old-fashioned tea-parties." In the case of the rows on the "little ladylike squares", "it was as if the virtuous dames had drawn together round a large green table; albeit to no more riotous end than that each should sit before her individual game of patience.*[66]*"*

•

*The typical rowhouse layout changed slightly at this time, as the plan of 1412 Park Avenue, constructed in 1857, illustrates. There was still a narrow passage with a side entrance between the front house and the rear wing. The double parlor became a long single parlor as the house became narrower. There was a porch on the back of the kitchen, as well as one above on the second floor. All houses were designed for efficiency and maximum ventilation: note the open passage from the front to the back of the house. A niche in the curving stair held statues, vases, etc., but was really for moving furniture up and coffins down. This house had gas lights and marble mantels in all the rooms except the top floor of bedrooms.*

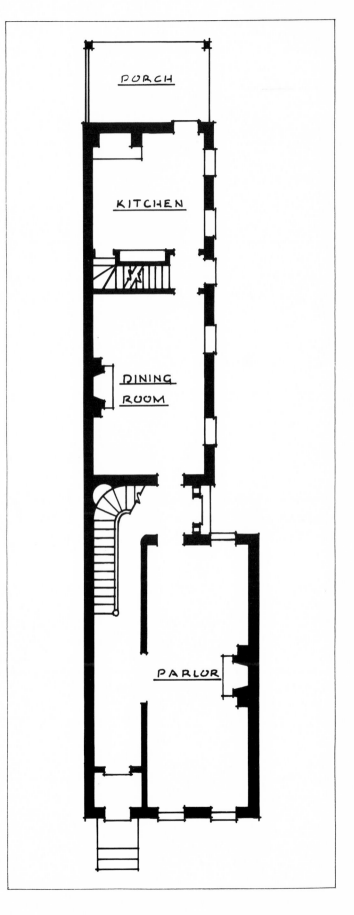

*Cast iron lintels were sometimes applied onto the sheer rowhouse facade during the Italianate phase.*

gave the silhouettes of the rows a new dynamism. Seen by the passerby at an angle, these bold details led the eye down a sweeping vista—contrasting with the timid profiles offered by earlier rows.

A century later, we can see how the Italianate style was incorporated into the Baltimore rowhouse tradition without breaking its continuity. The rowhouse's innate modesty prevailed, although the introduction of Italianate elements diluted some of the characteristic severity and restraint. Although elements of foreign character began creeping in—exterior decoration or brownstone rows—they did not have a wide or deep visual impact for a long time. Ornament, for example, seemed applied onto, rather than integrated into, the facade. These new features seemed mere acknowledgements of fashion more than something that constituted actual change in the form.

Those who regarded the Italianate style from a closer historical perspective, however, saw its advent as the beginning of the demise of the Baltimore style. J.B. Noel Wyatt wrote in 1895:

*With the close of the period of the "classic portico" about the middle of the century, even the most friendly spirit of criticism must turn to all that follows for the next twenty-five years with shame, and acknowledge not only that it finds no place for commendation, but rather that the kindest charity might say, in all that was done, there was really nothing to criticize.*[67]

*Cast iron railings, balconies, and fences, like these in the 900 block of North Fremont Avenue near Lafayette Square, enriched the facades of some Italianate rowhouses. Still, their patterns were generally more delicate than those popular in other cities.*

Changes crept in slowly after the middle of the 19th century. It may have been that there were no forces in Baltimore advocating change or that Baltimore preferred what it had already to what other cities were doing. Also, Baltimore's southernness may have impeded it from industrializing as rapidly as northern cities did and, consequently, its aesthetic response was less than whole-hearted. It must be noted, however, that the city was not oblivious to fashion. Residential squares, ornamental details, and locally-produced furniture kept pace with New York's stylistic innovations. Baltimore just did not find reason to change the character of its rowhouse in a major way. Romantic revivals, like the Gothic Revival of the 1840's, held little appeal for the city. Some Baltimoreans feel that the city was not dissatisfied enough with the 19th century to look to other eras for comfort.[68]

The lack of initiative in the development of the rowhouse is symptomatic of Baltimore's general lack of social focus. Until the 1850's a majority of the population was not native to the city. Because of Baltimore's youth, society as Philadelphia and Boston knew it had not had time to develop until mid-century. This social phenomenon was manifested in the lack of a single fashionable quarter. Grand rows appeared simultaneously in several areas of the city: Waverly Terrace and Franklin Square, Mt. Vernon Place,

Eutaw Place, Lafayette Square, the Battle Monument Square. As J.B. Noel Wyatt wrote, "The best class of houses was scattered. There was no one street of special interest and local pride.[69]"

The same dispersion of focus characterized the rowhouse. There were tentative embracings of styles, but none with any conviction. The houses of the rich showed the hesitancy more keenly. Builders meanwhile continued in the mode they knew well and knew would sell. The most conspicuous stylistic features showed up on the common rowhouses, but nothing that deviated dramatically from custom.

# The Demise of the Baltimore Rowhouse: 1870-1890

In any case, social forces held substantial change at bay until the end of the 19th century. The rowhouse changed little for the first two decades after the Civil War. Some people feel that the War disoriented Baltimore, forcing the city to retrench psychologically and reinforce its traditions. As one native noted:

*The war had deprived Baltimore of a clear model. No longer sure where its true interests lay — but certain that neither the [profit-making] convulsions nor the dead ruins of Richmond offered attractive choices — Baltimore was thrown back upon itself. Only Baltimore had any relevance to Baltimore, "the only world that mattered.[70]"*

---

*With industrialization came a democratized interior as well as exterior. Mass production allowed many people to have luxuries that had been available to only a few previously. Ceiling modillions, carved balusters and newel posts, gas chandeliers, shutters, bathrooms, round-headed double doors with glass panels to allow light into the hall, mantels of boldly-carved rococo forms or slate mantels painted to look like marble, became common in rowhouses of this period. Still, in Baltimore, although elaborate forms were available, the simpler versions were generally preferred, as the Illustrated Price List published in 1879 by George O. Stevens, a Baltimore firm, indicates. Stoves set in fireplaces were still used to heat the house. The Latrobe stove, invented in Baltimore by John H. B. Latrobe, heated several rooms by means of pipes run to fireplaces above.*

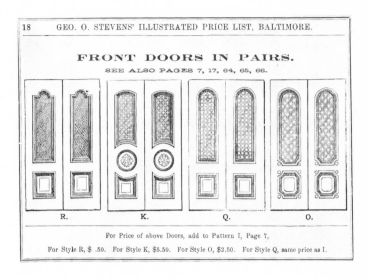

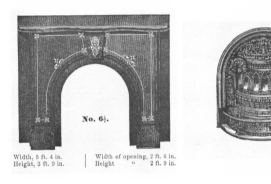

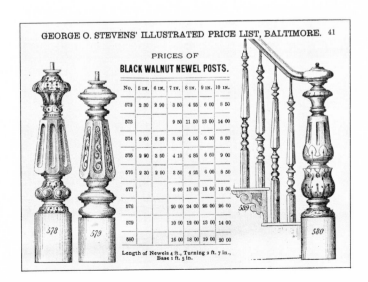

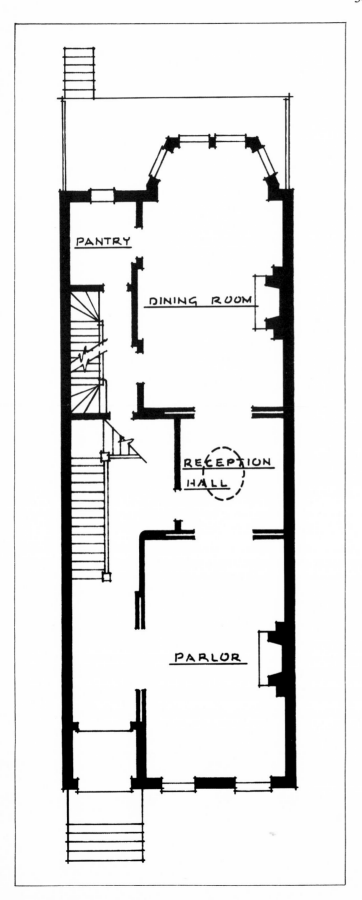

PANTRY

DINING ROOM

RECEPTION HALL

PARLOR

*During the post-Civil War period, floor plans grew increasingly grand, as this plan of 1617 Bolton Street, built in 1874, demonstrates. Sliding doors in the parlor and dining room opened the house "en filade". More adaptations were made to let light and ventilation into the center of the house. The reception hall was open to the roof, where there was an oval skylight, through which light could reach the bedrooms and bathrooms on either side of the well. Interior windows allowed cross-ventilation between these rooms. Bay windows and increased ceiling heights also made rooms lighter and airier. The roof of the basement kitchen areaway served as a balcony off the dining room, access to which was through floor-length windows. Central heating was introduced, rising from the coal furnace in the cellar through registers in the floors, although fireplaces with coal grates were still used. The pantry contained a dumbwaiter to the kitchen below. Woodwork was generally dark walnut, and walnut floors alternated with pine throughout the house. Etched glass was set in the front doors as well as the interior sliding doors. The living and dining rooms had plaster ceiling modillions and marble mantels.[71]*

*As professional architects were increasingly responsible for rowhouse design, the typical Baltimore rowhouse lost favor to rows like the Queen Anne-style Belvidere Terrace. Located in the 1000 block of North Calvert Street, this row was designed by J. B. Noel Wyatt in 1876.* ⟵

*Even the products of local builders showed signs of major change in the last quarter of the 19th century. The restraint typical of Baltimore was lost as gables broke up the even roofline and elaborate brickwork destroyed the planar facades.* ⟶

Baltimore's peculiar provinciality, i.e. its attitude that its boundaries contained all it needed to sustain itself, was reinforced at this time.

For both the North and the South, the War meant a clear break from the past. For the North, it marked an age of innovation, progress, and profit: new methods of education, moneymaking, and housing. Rowhouses adopted a spectrum of styles in an attempt to find one suitable for the new age. Baltimore was too close to the South to share fully in this innovating spirit. It did not benefit from a wartime boom, nor did it suffer from a drastic post-War depression. Baltimore did not change much because it had neither the catharsis of industrialization nor of destruction. Its own ambiguous position enforced its insularity, its solidarity, and its self-absorption. Post-War circumstances determined the continuity of the traditional rowhouse.

Speculative building was rampant after the Civil War. Scale of construction, standardization of parts, and new techniques cheapened and improved the basic rowhouse, so that even the cheapest houses had central heating and mass-produced Italianate ornament. In middle class houses, there were structural adaptations to allow more light and ventilation: skylights let light into the central core of the building and windows opened between rooms in the interior of the house. The Victorian penchant for creating buffer zones between rooms for privacy with hallways, vestibules, or areaways, also dictated some changes in the floor plan.

By the 1880's the rest of the country's eclecticism had infiltrated Baltimore's aesthetic. Two reasons for this lapse were: one, the development of the professional architect who took over rowhouse design from the master-builders; and two, the advent of illustrated

magazines. Their improved methods of reproduction of drawings allowed more precise renderings, so their visual influence was more intensive and practical. Also, as these magazines were able to report (or make) fashions more quickly, the time lag between innovation and popularization diminished. The result was a nationalization of styles.

*American Building News, New York Sketchbook of Architects,* and English magazines of the same genre with examples of the work of Richard Norman Shaw, William Butterfield et al, provided numerous prototypes for the designs of Baltimore buildings. Accordingly, rowhouses were given treatments that previously had been reserved for detached houses. Brickwork, whose evenness and simplicity had been Baltimore's trademark, became much more elaborate in the 1880's. Roman brick (long and narrow) or hard-glazed brown brick were especially popular. Various textural effects

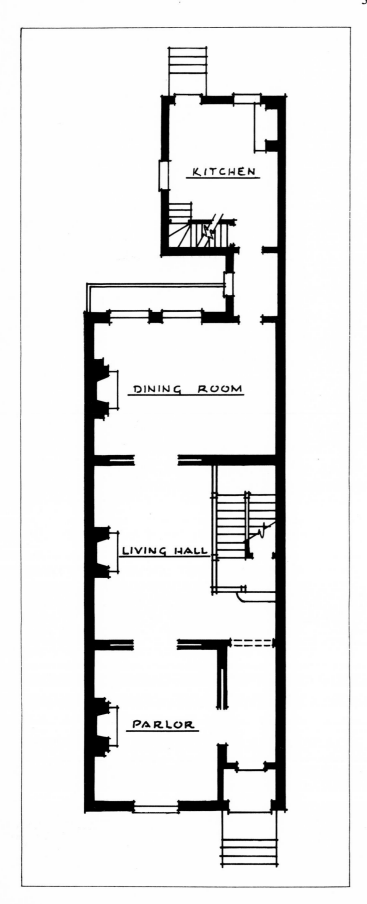

*The Romanesque brick and stone exterior of 2019 Maryland Avenue is indicative of the dissolution of the Baltimore rowhouse plan as well. The side hall became truncated, as the main staircase was incorporated into the center of the three main rooms. The staircase itself became more complicated, its wide landings and several changes of direction trying to do on a small scale what staircases in suburban houses did on a large scale. The kitchen, however, remained in a rear projection reminiscent of the traditional back building. Now the family sat in the living hall, while the parlor was reserved for formal occasions. There was a small balcony off the dining room, and a wooden grill of turned spindles or fretwork separated the entrance hall from the living hall. The woodwork was oak, and the mantels wood with tile surrounds and coal grates.[72]*

were simulated. Window size shrank, decorated gables rose up from the cornice, and forms protruded from the previously two-dimensional facade. The planarity and geometry were lost. Sometimes facades swelled into two-to-three story bays, and the cornice was ornamented with tile and cast iron. In 1895, J.B. Noel Wyatt lamented that the Baltimore type had "entirely disappeared from among the erections of recent years.[73]"

The breed of the traditional craftsmen-builders became nearly extinct. The economic and stylistic climate fostered the system of professional architects who designed rowhouses individually or large builders who constructed rowhouses by the mile. Prominent builders of the latter type were: Ephraim Macht, who came to Baltimore in 1886 and was responsible for many of the rowhouses on York Road, Park Heights Avenue, and in Liberty Heights; Matthew Mueller; Edward J. Gallagher, who built 8000 houses, mostly in East Baltimore; Frank Novak, who built in northeast Baltimore, Clifton Park, and Harford Road; James Kielty, who constructed 6000 houses in West Baltimore and Edmonson; and Joseph Bosse and Edward Storch, who worked in Upper Peabody Heights, now Charles Village.[74]

The exodus to the suburbs and the nationalization of styles were the two major factors in the demise of the traditional Baltimore rowhouse. The working class still lived in rowhouses after the turn of the century, but the middle and upper classes no longer found them suitable for their needs. Public transportation allowed

*This row in Highlandtown, typical of those built by the mile by speculative builders in the early 20th century, shows that the Baltimore type did not disappear entirely. Indeed, it illustrates graphically local architectural historian Phoebe Stanton's description of Baltimore's rows: "Constructed on the building line, raised from the street level on a stone or marble base, organized into long walls composed of the tall vertical rectangles of the undeclarative house fronts punctuated by the repetitive patterns of windows, doors, and cornices. . .as severe and undecorative as a machine, each front an understated shell to enclose the standard but useful rowhouse plan within.*[75]*"

people to move out of the city—out of walking range of their work and society. Healthier climates were now accessible, and whoever could take advantage of them did.

In its rowhouse, Baltimore evolved a vernacular architecture that is a symbol of the city. The rowhouse adapted to local topography, climate, economics, and traditions. Its attenuated proportions, elegant facades, and arrangement in rows on broad hilly streets, created a serene and enduring beauty. Oblivious to passing styles, the form evolved gradually and steadfastly—directed by a combination of social, economic, and perhaps least of all, aesthetic forces that allowed few diversions.

Although the rowhouse was one of the first signals that Baltimore was to become an urban center in the 18th century, by the middle of the 19th century it signified the city's conservatism and its determination

not to match the pace of other cities. Industrialization propelled many cities into a new era. But Baltimore continued to build the traditional type of housing in the traditional style. It thus maintained its equilibrium while many other cities experienced major upheavals. The lines of rows symbolized Baltimore's way of dealing with progress.

At the beginning of the 20th century, the mayor of Baltimore applauded the "wholesome" effect of the "individual homes for each individual.[76]" Letitia Stockett wrote in 1936 of "the quiet and sense of withdrawal", "the small-town atmosphere" of the neighborhoods.[77] Rowhouses always maintained a human scale and control in Baltimore; other cities succumbed to the delusion that bigger was better. As one British newsman said on a visit to Baltimore in 1893, "You feel that it is always afternoon here. . . thankful so quiet a city is to be found in the same country which contains New York and Chicago.[78]"

# Notes

1. H. L. Mencken, *The Vintage Mencken,* edited by Alistair Cooke, p.202.
2. Hubert Hoffman, *Rowhouses and Cluster Houses,* p.12.
3. John Dorsey and James Dilts, *A Guide to Baltimore Architecture,* p.156.
4. Vincent Scully, *American Architecture and Urbanism,* p.83.
5. Louis Simond, quoted in John Summerson, *Georgian London,* p.15.
6. Stephen Gardiner, *Evolution of the House,* p.156.
7. James Fenimore Cooper, quoted in Charles Lockwood, *Bricks and Brownstone,* p.7.
8. Robert Eney, interview, January, 1978.
9. Jane Garrett, "Philadelphia and Baltimore, 1790-1840," *Maryland Historical Magazine,* Vol. 55, No. 1, p.6.
10. T. Worth Jamison, "The Early Architecture of Baltimore," Baltimore *Sunpapers,* September 8, 1930.
11. Esther Eckels, "Early Baltimore Architects," pp.61,123.
12. Kenneth Ames, "Robert Mills and the Philadelphia Rowhouse," *Journal for the Society of Architectural Historians,* Vol. 27, No. 2, p.143.
13. Robert F. Alexander, "William F. Small, Architect of the City," *Journal for the Society of Architectural Historians,* p.243.
14. Robert Smith, "John Hall, A Busy Man in Baltimore," *Antiques,* p.363.
15. Robert Raley, "The Baltimore Country House," p.41.
16. The list of names came from three sources: Spencer and Howland's *The Architecture of Baltimore,* pp.20-21; Robert Raley's "The Baltimore Country House," p.50; and Esther Eckels' "Early Architects of Baltimore," pp.42, 45.
17. Wilbur Hunter, *Maryland Heritage,* edited by John Boles, p.231.
18. Francis Beirne, *Baltimore: A Picture History,* p.17.
19. Spencer and Howland, *The Architecture of Baltimore,* p.117.
20. Thomas Twining, quoted in Rodris Roth, "Interior Decoration of City Houses in Baltimore," *Winterthur Portfolio,* no. 5, p.64.
21. John Harriott, quoted in Roth, "Interior Decoration," p.62.
22. Sherry Olson, *Baltimore,* p.7.
23. Nicholas Pevsner, *Studies in Art, Architecture, and Design,* p.115.
24. Dorsey and Dilts, *Guide,* p.xxxiv.
25. Letitia Stockett, *Baltimore, a Not Too Serious History,* p.42.
26. Gerald W. Johnson, quoted in John Schmidt, "Houses that have shaped a way of life," Baltimore *Sun,* February 17, 1963.
27. Olson, *Baltimore,* p.220.
28. J.B. Noel Wyatt, "Baltimore Architecture," in *Baltimore, The Old Town . . . and . . . The Modern City,* p.167.
29. F. Scott Fitzgerald, *Afternoon of an Author,* p.101.
30. John Schmidt, "Our Famous White Marble Steps," Baltimore *Sun,* March 24, 1963.
31. Schmidt, "Marble Steps."
32. Dorsey and Dilts, *Guide,* p.4.
33. Wyatt, "Baltimore Architecture," p.174.
34. Stockett, *Not Too Serious History,* p.230.
35. H.L. Mencken, Baltimore *Evening Sun,* February 27, 1927.
36. Montgomery Schuyler, "The Small City House in New York," *The Architectural Record,* April-June, 1899.
37. Eckels, "Baltimore Architects," p.8.
38. Olson, *Baltimore,* p.41.
39. Quoted in Roth, "Interior Decoration," p.63.
40. Phoebe Stanton, Poppleton study, p.29.
41. Roth, "Interior Decoration," p.64.
42. Wyatt, "Baltimore Architecture," p.153.
43. Michael Trostel, interview, December, 1978.
44. Quoted in Roth, "Interior Decoration," p.64.
45. Except as noted, information on Federal interiors presented here found in Roth, "Interior Decoration."
46. Quoted in Spencer and Howland, *The Architecture of Baltimore,* p.6.
47. HABS data sheets.
48. Wyatt, "Baltimore Architecture," p.161.
49. Wyatt, "Baltimore Architecture," p.161.
50. Wyatt, "Baltimore Architecture," p.162.
50.a The plan of the Joshua Cohen house (p.13), 1830, placed the kitchen in the basement and the dining room and breakfast room on the first floor. The heights of the Cohen house rooms illustrate the grander proportions of these houses: first floor rooms were 13' 1"; second floor rooms 11'3"; and third floor rooms 10'3".
51. Talbot Hamlin, *Greek Revival Architecture in America,* p.189.
52. Stanton, Poppleton, p.32.

53. Spencer and Howland, *The Architecture of Baltimore,* p.110.
54. Smith, "John Hall," p. 148.
55. Quoted in Lockwood, *Bricks and Brownstone,* p.128.
56. Lockwood, *Bricks and Brownstone,* p.128.
57. Stanton, Poppleton, p.34.
58. Olson, *Baltimore,* pp.112-113.
59. Olson, *Baltimore,* p.114.
60. Lockwood, *Bricks and Brownstone,* p.153.
61. Quoted in Lockwood, *Bricks and Brownstone,* p.153.
62. Quoted in Lockwood, *Bricks and Brownstone,* p.151.
63. Olson, *Baltimore,* p.290.
64. Quoted in Stanton, Poppleton, p.42.
65. George Frederick, notes in vertical file, Maryland Historical Society.
66. Henry James, *The American Scene,* p.311.
67. Wyatt, "Baltimore Architecture," p.164.
68. Interview with Charles Duff, January, 1978.
69. Wyatt, "Baltimore Architecture," p.168.
70. Duff interview.
71. Trostel interview.
72. Trostel interview.
73. Wyatt, "Baltimore Architecture," p.161.
74. Jacques Kelly, interview, January, 1978.
75. Phoebe Stanton, "Keeping the 'There' in Baltimore," Baltimore *Evening Sun,* April 5, 1968.
76. Quoted in Olson, *Baltimore,* p.272.
77. Stockett, *Not Too Serious History,* p.22.
78. Quoted in Olson, PhD thesis, p.477.

# Illustrations

# Bibliography

*Books*

Beirne, Francis, *The Amiable Baltimoreans.* New York: E. P. Dutton, 1951.
Beirne, Francis (commentary), *Baltimore: A Picture History.* Baltimore: Bodine, 1968.
Bennett, George Fletcher, *Early Architecture of Delaware.* Wilmington, New York, 1932.
Black, Mary, *Old New York in Early Photographs 1853 - 1901.* New York: Dover Publications, 1973.
Boles, John B, ed., *Maryland Heritage.* Baltimore: Maryland Historical Society, 1976.
Bunting, Bainbridge, *Houses of Boston's Back Bay.* Cambridge: Belknap Press, 1967.
Cooke, Alistair, ed., *The Vintage Mencken.* New York: Vintage Books, div. of Alfred A. Knopf, Inc., ©1955.
Cooney, Robert F., *Old Philadelphia in Early Photographs 1839 - 1914.* New York: Dover Publications, 1976.
Cruikshank, Dan, and Wyld, Peter, *The Art of Georgian Building.* London: The Architectural Press, Ltd., 1977.
Dorsey, John, and Dilts, James D., *A Guide to Baltimore Architecture.* Cambridge, Md.: Tidewater Publishers, 1981.
Elwell, Newton W., *The Architecture, Furniture and Interiors of Maryland and Virginia during the 18th Century.* Boston: G. H. Polley and Co., c. 1897.
Gardiner, Stephen, *Evolution of the House.* New York: Macmillan, 1974.
Goldstone, Harmon Henricks, and Dalrymple, Martha, *History Preserved: A Guide to New York Landmarks and Historic Districts.* New York: Simon & Schuster, 1974.
Hall, John, *A Series of Select and Original Modern Designs for the Use of Carpenters and Builders Adapted to the Style of Building in the United States.* Baltimore: John Murphy, 1840.
Hamlin, Talbot, *Greek Revival Architecture in America.* New York: Dover Publications, 1964.
Hoffman, Hubert, *Rowhouses and Cluster Houses: An International Survey.* New York: Praeger, 1967.
Howland, Richard, and Spencer, Eleanor, *The Architecture of Baltimore.* Baltimore: Johns Hopkins Press, ©1953.
Hughes, T. H., and Lamborn, E.A.G., *Town and Town Planning: Ancient and Modern.* Oxford: Oxford University Press, 1923.
Hunter, Wilbur H., and Elam, Charles H., *Century of Baltimore Architecture.* Baltimore: Peale Museum, 1957.
Jackson, Joseph, *Development of American Architecture 1783 - 1830.* Philadelphia: David McKay, 1926.
James, Henry, *The American Scene.* Bloomington: Indiana University Press, 1968.
Kelly, Jacques, *Peabody Heights to Charles Village.* Baltimore: The Equitable Trust Co., 1976.
Lafever, Minard, *The Modern Builders Guide.* New York: Daniel Burgess & Co., 1853.
Lancaster, Clay, *Old Brooklyn Heights.* Rutland, Vt.: Charles E. Tuttle Co., 1960.
Lockwood, Charles, *Bricks and Brownstone.* New York: McGraw - Hill, 1972.
McCall, Elizabeth B., *Old Philadelphia Houses on Society Hill 1750 - 1840.* New York: Architectural Book Publishers, 1966.
McCauley, Lois B., *Maryland Historical Prints 1752 - 1899.* Baltimore: Maryland Historical Society, 1975.
Olsen, Donald J., *Town Planning in London.* New Haven: Yale University Press, 1964.
Olson, Sherry, *Baltimore, the Building of an American City.* Baltimore: The Johns Hopkins University Press, 1980.
Pevsner, Nicholas, *Studies in Art, Architecture, and Design.* New York: McGraw - Hill, 1968, Vol. II.
Richardson & Gill, *London Houses from 1660 - 1820.* London: B. T. Batsford, 1958.
Scully, Vincent, *American Architecture and Urbanism.* New York: Praeger Publishers, Inc.,©1969, permission Holt, Rinehart, & Winston.
Sloan, Samuel, *City and Suburban Architect.* Philadelphia: J.B. Lippincott & Co., 1859.
Stockett, Letitia, *Baltimore: A Not Too Serious History.* Baltimore: Grace Gore Norman, 1936.
Summerson, John, *Georgian London.* New York: Scribners, 1946.
Tatum, George B., *Philadelphia Georgian.* Middletown: Wesleyan University Press, 1976.
Waite, Diana S., ed., *Architectural Elements, The Technological Revolution.* Princeton: The Pyne Press, 1960.
Wyatt, J.B., "Baltimore Architecture" in *Baltimore, The Old Town...and...The Modern City,* Souvenir of the 9th Convention of the National Association of Builders, 1895.
Yerbery, F.R., ed., *Old Domestic Architecture of Holland.* London: The Architectural Press, 1924.
Zucker, Paul, *Town and Square, From the Agora to the Village Square.* Cambridge: MIT Press, 1959.


*Periodicals*

Alexander, Robert L., "The Cosmopolitan Style of Latrobe and Godefroy," *Maryland Historical Magazine,* Vol. 56, no. 3.
Alexander, Robert L., "Baltimore Row Houses of the Early Nineteenth Century," *American Studies XVI,* pp. 65-76.
Alexander, Robert L., "William F. Small, Architect of the City," *Journal of the Society of Architectural Historians,* Vol. 20, no. 2, pp. 63 - 77.
Ames, Kenneth, "Robert Mills and the Philadelphia Rowhouse," *Journal of the Society of Architectural Historians,* Vol. 27, no. 2, pp. 140 - 146.

Carter, Edward C., III, "The Papers of Benjamin H. Latrobe and the Maryland Historical Society 1885 - 1971: Nature, Structure, and Acquisition," *Maryland Historical Magazine,* Vol. 66, no. 4.

Cox, Richard J., and Vanorny, Patricia M., "The Records of a City: Baltimore and its Historical Sources," *Maryland Historical Magazine,* Vol. 70, no. 3.

Elder, William Voss, "Robert Mills' Waterloo Row — Baltimore 1816," *The Record,* Vol. 1, no. 12 (Pamphlet published by the Baltimore Museum of Art).

Garrett, Jane N., "Philadelphia and Baltimore, 1790 - 1840: A Study of Intraregional Unity," *Maryland Historical Magazine,* Vol. 55, no. 1.

Hamlin, Talbot, "Benjamin Henry Latrobe: The Man and the Architect," *Maryland Historical Magazine,* Vol. 37, no. 4.

Latrobe, Ferdinand C., II, "Benjamin H. Latrobe: Descent and Works," *Maryland Historical Magazine,* Vol. 33, no. 3.

Murtagh, William John, "The Philadelphia Row House," *Journal of the Society of Architectural Historians,* Vol. 16, no. 4, pp. 8 - 13.

Roth, Rodris, "Interior Decoration of City Houses in Baltimore: The Federal Period," *Winterthur Portfolio #5,* University of Virginia Press, 1969.

Schuyler, Montgomery, "The Small City House in New York," *The Architectural Record,* Vol. 8, April - June, 1899.

Smith, Robert C., "John Hall, A Busy Man in Baltimore," *Antiques,* September, 1967.

Whitney, Henry, "Baltimore Row Houses," *Architectural Forum,* May, 1957.

*Newspapers*

Arnett, Earl, "Cityscape 'A Humane Scale', " *Sunpapers,* August 20, 1968.

Beirne, Francis, "Baltimore's Story of Architecture," *Sunpapers,* March 13 - May 1, 1927.

Dorsey, John, "Mount Vernon Place," *Sun Magazine,* June 7, 1970.

Jamison, T. Worth, "The Early Architecture of Baltimore," *Sunpapers,* September 8, 1930.

Lyon, Helen K., "Atlanta's Old Baltimore Place Still Stands as Example of Early Housing Endeavor," *Sunpapers,* November 7, 1959.

McCardell, Lee, "Those Rows of White Steps in City — They're a 'Mark of Respectability'," *Sunpapers,* September 11, 1951.

Mencken, H.L., *Evening Sun,* February 27, 1927.

Schmidt, John, "Houses That Have Shaped a Way of Life," *Sunpapers,* February 17, 1963.

Schmidt, John, "Our Famous White Marble Steps, Status Symbols," *Sunpapers,* February 24, 1963.

Stanton, Phoebe, "Keeping the 'There' in Baltimore," *Evening Sun,* April 5, 1968.

*Unpublished Sources*

Eckels, Esther Wittler, "Baltimore's Earliest Architects," thesis submitted to the Johns Hopkins University, 1950. (On deposit at Johns Hopkins University library.)

Olson, Sherry, "The History of Baltimore," thesis submitted to the Johns Hopkins University, 1976. (On deposit at Commission for Historic and Architectural Preservation, Baltimore.)

Raley, Robert, "The Baltimore Country House," thesis submitted to the University of Delaware, 1959. (On deposit at the Winterthur library.)

Stanton, Phoebe, Study of the Poppleton area, under the aegis of HCD, 1975. (On deposit at Commission for Historic and Architectural Preservation, Baltimore.)

# *About the Author ...*

Natalie Wilkins Shivers writes with a strong background in urban design and architectural history. The basis of *Those Old Placid Rows* was her senior thesis for Yale University, which was awarded the Mark Dietz Memorial Prize for original research in art history. After she graduated from Yale in 1978, she worked as an architectural historian for the Maryland Historical Trust in Harford County. She has assisted the Savannah Landmark Rehabilitation Project in Savannah, Georgia, and the Irish Georgian Society in County Cork, Ireland. Ms. Shivers is currently studying architecture at Princeton University.

*Printed by Peabody Press, Inc.*